Contents

Some words are shown in bold, **like this**. You can find out what they mean by looking in the glossary.

The Variety of Life

The natural world is full of an incredible variety of **organisms**. They range from tiny **bacteria**, too small to see, to giant redwood trees over 100 meters (328 feet) tall. With such a bewildering variety of life, it's hard to make sense of the living world. For this reason, scientists **classify** living things by sorting them into groups.

Classifying the living world

Sorting organisms into groups makes them easier to understand. Scientists try to classify living things in a way that tells you how closely one group is related to another. They look at everything about an organism, from its color and shape to the **genes** inside its **cells**. They even look at **fossils** to give them clues about how living things have changed over time. Then the scientists use all this information to sort the millions of different things into groups.

Scientists don't always agree about the group an organism belongs to, so they collect as much evidence as possible to find its closest relatives.

Flowering plants come in many sizes and shapes. You can see tulips and purple hyacinths in this flower garden.

From kingdoms to species

Classification allows us to measure the **biodiversity** of the world. To begin the classification process, scientists divide living things into huge groups called **kingdoms**. For example, plants are in one kingdom, while animals are in another. There is some argument among scientists about how many kingdoms there are—at the moment most agree that there are five! Each kingdom is then divided into smaller groups called **phyla** (singular phylum), and the phyla are further divided into **classes**. The next subdivision is into **orders**. Within an order, organisms are grouped into **families** and then into a **genus** (plural genera), which contains a number of closely related **species**. A species is a single kind of organism, such as a mouse or a buttercup. Members of a species can **reproduce** and produce fertile offspring together.

Scientific names

Many living things have a common name, but these can cause confusion when the same organism has different names around the world. To avoid problems, scientists give every species a two-part Latin name, which is the same all over the world. The first part of the scientific name tells you the genus the organism belongs to. The second part tells you the exact species. The plains or Canadian prickly pear cactus, for example, is *Opuntia polyacantha*, while the most common variety, Englemann's prickly pear, is *Opuntia engelmannii*.

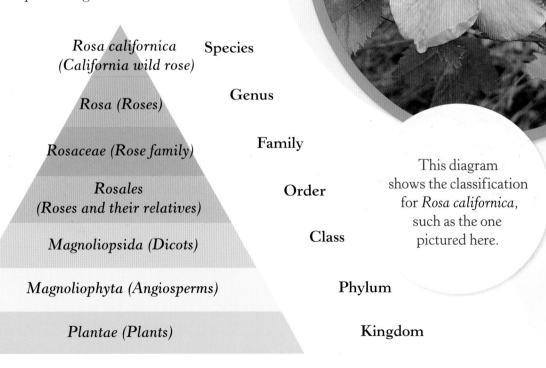

This diagram shows the classification for *Rosa californica*, such as the one pictured here.

Rosa californica
(California wild rose) — Species

Rosa (Roses) — Genus

Rosaceae (Rose family) — Family

Rosales
(Roses and their relatives) — Order

Magnoliopsida (Dicots) — Class

Magnoliophyta (Angiosperms) — Phylum

Plantae (Plants) — Kingdom

Flowering plants make up their own **division** in the plant **kingdom**. Flowering plants make **seeds** as well as flowers and **fruits**. There are two main kinds of seed plants within the flowering plant kingdom: **gymnosperms** and **angiosperms**.

Gymnosperms make "naked seeds," such as the seeds in a pine cone. Unlike fruits, pine cones open up and expose their seeds to the air when they are mature and the weather is good for growth. Gymnosperms are thought to be the **ancestors** of flowering plants.

Flowering plants are called angiosperms. Unlike gymnosperms, angiosperms enclose their seeds in fruits. Angiosperms are a very successful group of plants. In fact, they make up most of the plant kingdom. Of the approximately 300,000 living plant **species**, more than 250,000 belong to the angiosperm division. Most of the plants around you are angiosperms. Angiosperms grow almost everywhere on land—even in difficult growing conditions on the islands off the continent of Antarctica—and in many water environments. Orchids and bromeliads are usually found in tropical regions. Angiosperms live in more **habitats** than any other group of plants.

Gladiolus—common garden flower

- About 300 species
- Has a complete flower
- Flower grows from bulblike structure called a corm
- Name comes from a Latin word meaning "sword"

The structure of flowers

The parts of a flower can be divided into four circles or **whorls**. Small green **sepals**, which protect the bud, are the outer whorl. Petals make up the second whorl, with the male reproductive organs, called **stamens**, third, and the female reproductive organs, called **pistils**, on the inside.

Some flowers have all four whorls and are called **complete flowers**. Some don't have sepals, or only contain male or female parts. They are **incomplete flowers**. A flower with both male and female parts is called **perfect** even if it is incomplete. An **imperfect flower** has either stamens or pistils.

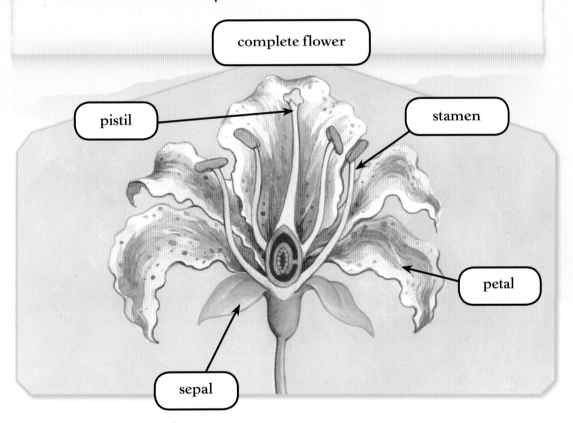

complete flower

pistil

stamen

petal

sepal

Pollinating flowers

For plants to **reproduce**, **pollen** needs to get from one flower to another flower. This is called **pollination**. Some flowers have bright colors or a strong scent. Colors, patterns, scents, and **nectar** (a sugary liquid) are some of the ways that flowers attract insects or other animals to them. As the animals drink the nectar, they may get coated in pollen, which they then carry to another flower. This is insect (or animal) pollination, which, for example, occurs in apple trees.

Other plants have small, greenish flowers with dangling stamens and lots of light pollen. They rely on the wind blowing the pollen away to other plants. This is wind pollination, which, for example, occurs in grass.

Fruits

A **fruit** is the ripened female reproductive part of the flower. Fruits protect the **seeds**, which contain the new baby plants. They also help them travel to new places. The fruits of flowering plants are vitally important to us—and to other animals—as food.

Some flowering plants, such as dandelions and maples, have seeds in fruits shaped like kites, parachutes, or propellers, which are carried on the wind to new places. Other flowering plants have fruits with hooks or hairs that attach to animal fur or human clothing and get carried from place to place. Many plants have seeds in fruits that are good to eat. The seeds are deposited in a new place when they pass through the **digestive system** complete with ready-made manure!

The seeds of dandelions are in fruits shaped like tiny parachutes. The wind carries these seeds away. When the seed reaches a new place suitable for growing, it grows into a new dandelion plant.

The body of a flowering plant has three main parts: roots, stems, and leaves. Each part has a specific function to help the plant survive.

Roots

Roots are usually the part of a plant that grows under the ground. Roots hold a plant in place. Roots also take in water and **minerals** from the soil around them. The roots then pass the water and minerals on to the plant's stem. The roots of some plants store food for the plant.

Roots grow only from their ends. The tip of a root is covered with a little protective cap. The root cap protects the root as it grows through dirt.

Stems

Stems do not always look alike, but you can usually recognize them because they are growing up from the ground. **Angiosperm** stems usually have flowers and leaves or branches growing out from them. The trunk of a tree is a stem. The main stalk of a plant connecting the plant's roots and its leaves is also a stem.

The roots, stems, and leaves of a plant all work toward the production of flowers, which enables the whole **organism** to **reproduce**.

9

Stems move water and **nutrients** from one part of a plant to its other parts. Some green stems also make food by the process of **photosynthesis**. Other stems store food. For example, potatoes are underground stems, called **tubers**. Some stems, such as those on rose bushes, have thorns on them. Thorns help protect a plant from animals. The stems of cactuses are usually thick and can store water.

Leaves

Leaves are usually flat and green. They grow out from stems. Leaves carry out photosynthesis and make food for the entire plant. Not all leaves look alike. Some leaf **adaptations** allow plants to climb, store water or nutrients, fend off **predators**, trap and **digest prey**, or adjust to **climate**. For example, the leaves on a cactus are long spikes. These spikes prevent animals from eating the plant. They also collect water in the form of dew. The dew forms on the spikes and drips to the ground. Then it soaks into the ground and the cactus's roots take it in. Other plant leaves, such as those on aloe and hen-and-chick plants, are thick and store water.

Cactuses are native to North and South America and are adapted to dry areas. Their thick stems are usually green and carry out photosynthesis. They may have no leaves, or just small spines instead of green leaves. Their thin roots grow close to the surface of the ground, where they take in water from dew and occasional rains. Most scientists think that the cactuses growing in other parts of the world were brought there from North and South America.

There are about 250,000 living **species** of **angiosperms**. They are grouped into two main **classes**: **monocots** and **dicots**.

Two classes of flowering plants

Flowering plants are divided into two classes based on how many seed leaves, or **cotyledons**, they have. Seed leaves are the leaves a plant grows when it is still an **embryo** inside a **seed**. Flowering plants with two seed leaves are called dicotyledons, or dicots. Those with only one seed leaf are called monocotyledons, or monocots.

The orders

Monocot and dicot classes are divided into **orders**. There are many orders of flowering plants. Dicots are usually divided into about 50 orders. Monocots are divided into 10–15 orders. Only some of these orders are discussed here. To learn more, you might talk to a gardener or join a gardening club. You can also learn a lot about flowering plants at a nearby botanical garden or arboretum.

	Monocots	Dicots
Seed leaves	one seed leaf e.g., corn seed	two seed leaves e.g., bean seed
Flowers	flower parts in multiples of four or five e.g., day lily	flower parts in multiples of three e.g., evening primrose
Leaf veins	leaf veins are parallel e.g., grass leaf	leaf veins form a net pattern e.g., maple leaf
Roots	fibrous roots e.g., grass root	taproot e.g., dandelion root
Examples	corn, day lily, iris, wheat, camas	bean, rose, sunflower, violet, maple, water lily

Magnolias, paw paw, and nutmeg are related to the earliest-known flowering plants. These plants tend to be either woody bushes, climbing plants, or trees. They are grouped together in the magnolia **order** mainly because they have some ancient features that plants in other orders no longer have.

All members of this group are **dicots**—they have two seed leaves. Members of this group are found all over the world. They live in both wet and dry areas. Some have leaves that are coated with wax. The wax helps keep water inside the plant.

The world's oldest flowering plant

The oldest known flowering plant lived 140 million years ago. A **fossil** of this **extinct** plant was found in China. Some scientists think that this plant grew in shallow water at the same time that dinosaurs lived on Earth.

The first-known flowering plants are related to today's magnolia trees. If you live in the southeastern part of the United States, then you might have seen or smelled a magnolia tree. These trees make very strong, sweet-smelling flowers. But the oldest flowering plants did not look like magnolia trees at all. Their flowers did not even have petals. Their **seeds** were enclosed in flowering structures that may have developed like magnolias.

Magnolia **fruits** are shaped like cones. Their seeds are often red and hang by threads.

Oak trees belong to the oak order within the dicots. The leaves on these trees have netlike **veins**, which is a characteristic of dicots. Most of the members of this group are common flowering trees, for example oak and hazelnut. The flowers on these trees tend to be small and green.

Falling leaves

You have probably noticed that some trees, such as oaks, lose their leaves in the fall. These trees are called **deciduous** trees. Deciduous trees stop growing in winter. This helps them to avoid drying out since roots cannot get water from frozen ground. By dropping leaves, the trees avoid water loss through their leaves and keep more water inside the plant.

Related forms

Some orders, such as walnut, elm, and mulberry, are **classified** with oak because they tend to have separate male and female flowers.

Tree garlands

Oaks and most of their relatives are **pollinated** by wind. Wind carries the pollen from male flowers to female flowers. These flowers usually do not have an odor. Often the flowers are small. Many small male flowers form long, powdery chains called catkins that dangle from the trees. The small female flowers are found individually on the twigs. They have wide open stigmas to catch the pollen from the breeze.

Oak trees in the United States pollinate from February until June. During pollination, wind carries pollen many kilometers away from the male flowers in the catkins.

Insect-eating plants

You probably know that some insects eat plants. But did you know that some plants eat insects? There are about 200 **species** of meat-eating plants in the **dicots**. They include the Venus flytrap, the pitcher plant, and the sundew. They live in areas where the soil is poor. These plants use their leaves to trap insects. Trapping insects and absorbing **nutrients** from the insect bodies allows the plants to get nutrients that are not present in the soil.

Insect-eating plants have different ways of catching insects. Pitcher plants form a deep cup with their leaves. The hoodlike leaf that covers the deep cup gives off a strong smell that attracts insects. When the insects come to the leaf, they fall into the pitcher, where they are **digested**.

The leaves of a Venus flytrap form a snapping trap. Tiny hairs on the surface of the leaves signal the leaves to close around **prey** inside the trap. Digestive juices break down the insect's body and the plant absorbs the nutrients.

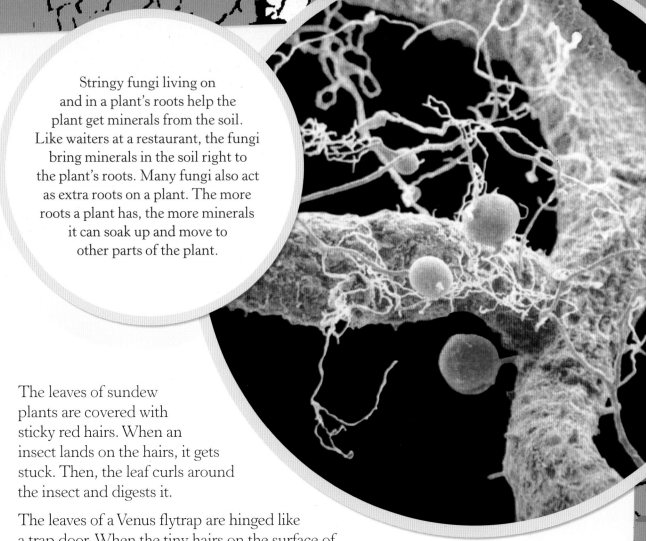

Stringy fungi living on and in a plant's roots help the plant get minerals from the soil. Like waiters at a restaurant, the fungi bring minerals in the soil right to the plant's roots. Many fungi also act as extra roots on a plant. The more roots a plant has, the more minerals it can soak up and move to other parts of the plant.

The leaves of sundew plants are covered with sticky red hairs. When an insect lands on the hairs, it gets stuck. Then, the leaf curls around the insect and digests it.

The leaves of a Venus flytrap are hinged like a trap door. When the tiny hairs on the surface of the leaves are touched, the leaves snap shut. This traps any insect that might have touched the leaves inside. The insect's body is digested inside the trap.

Fungi-friendly plants

Fungi live on the roots of some plants in this group. They include azaleas, rhododendrons, blueberries, and cranberries. Some of these plants cannot survive without fungi. Others can live without fungi, but they are healthier when the fungi live on and in their roots. Long threads of fungi grow all around and even inside the plant roots. The fungi and plant roots often look like a big tangle of string.

By living on or in the roots, the fungi and the roots are able to exchange food and **minerals**. The fungi get food from the plant's roots. Food that the plant makes by **photosynthesis** moves from the roots into the fungi. Fungi provides minerals from the soil directly to the plant's roots.

Another group of **dicots** is the rose and its related **orders**. Many plants related to roses are well known for their beauty or **fruit**. You might be surprised that many plants in this group do not look like roses.

The leaves on these plants usually have compound leaves. This means there is more than one leaf attached to each leaf stem. Their flowers usually have petals that are separated from one another. The flowers of roses and their relatives also tend to develop in the same way. Roses, apples, peaches, cherries, pears, plums, strawberries, and raspberries are all in this group.

Cultivated roses

Most roses that you see today are **cultivated** roses. These are roses that people have developed to produce specific kinds of flowers. The color of a plant's flowers is determined by the plant's **genes**. Roses do not usually have a gene for red or blue flower color. Australian and Japanese scientists have recently created a blue rose, but its color is very pale.

These are cultivated roses. They come in red, white, yellow, pink, orange, and lavender. No wild rose plants make red or blue flowers.

Parasitic Plants

Some plants do not make their own food by **photosynthesis**. These are the **parasitic** plants, and they get their **nutrients** by living off other plants. There are more than 4,000 species of parasitic plants. They range from plants that live completely within the tissues of other plants, such as the rafflesias, to plants that are green and photosynthesize but just "top off" their food needs from other plants. Parasitic plants can attack the roots, the stems, or the whole body of their **host**. They include some of the most bizarre members of the plant **kingdom**.

Do you know ... which flower smells like rotting meat?

The giant rafflesia makes the largest known flowers. They can be 1 meter (3 feet, 3 inches) wide — that's about as wide as a 3-year-old child is tall. These huge flowers smell like rotting meat. This smell attracts flies that **pollinate** the flowers. This stinky plant is **classified** in its own order. Unless you see one of the flowers of these parasites, you might never notice it at all. Rafflesia is a parasitic plant, and lives as a tangle of white threads within the body of the host plant, often a vine.

About 18,000 **species** of plants are legumes. Their flowers contain only one **pistil**. Their **fruits** are called pods. When ripe, the pod splits open and releases the **seeds**. Legumes make up another **order** of **dicots**.

Making food for you and me

If you have ever eaten peanut butter, then you have eaten the product of a legume. Legumes are important in the world for the production of food for humans and for animals that are raised to feed humans. Foods made from legumes are high in protein and fat. These **nutrients** are necessary for human growth. Peanuts, chick peas, lentils, soybeans, and other beans and peas are all foods from legume fruits. Alfalfa and clover are legumes used to feed animals.

Peas—one of the oldest cultivated crops
- Grown on vines
- Peas are the fruit of pea plants

Fixing nitrogen

Have you ever heard of someone **fertilizing** a plant? When you fertilize a plant, you give it nutrients, most importantly **nitrogen**, in a form it can use to grow. Legumes have their own fertilizer factories in their roots!

Legumes have swollen bumps on their roots where the **bacteria** live. These bacteria take nitrogen and change it into a form that plants can use to live and grow. Animals and other living things then get that nitrogen by eating plants.

Nitrogen-fixing bacteria live in these ball-shaped structures on the roots of legume plants. The plants give the bacteria a home and food. In return, the bacteria provide the plant and other living things with nitrogen.

Did you know ... legumes help us stay alive?

All living things need nitrogen to live. Nitrogen is used to make hair, skin, and fingernails. It is also an important part of **genetic** material. But most of the nitrogen in the world is in a form that living things cannot use. Nitrogen-fixing bacteria unlock this nitrogen. Without nitrogen-fixing bacteria, living things would run out of nitrogen. In this way, legume plants help all other plants and animals around them get nitrogen.

You have probably seen palms in movies, or maybe in person. Palms grow in warm, wet places, such as along beaches and in tropical areas. Their leaves are usually fan-shaped or feather-shaped. If you look closely at the leaves, you will notice that they have parallel **veins**. This and other characteristics of palms tell you that these plants are **monocots**. They make up an ancient **order** of plants that have lived on Earth for more than 110 million years.

Not real trees

You may have heard palms called "palm trees." Palms grow tall like trees, but they are not like other trees. A palm usually has a tall trunk that is about the same diameter from ground to "tree" top. In fact, the trunk often reaches its full width before the plant grows above ground. The trunks of most trees get wider each year, but the trunks of palms do not. Also unlike most trees, palms rarely have branches.

Palm flowers and fruits

Members of this group usually have small flowers. Many tiny flowers grow off one branch. Some palms grow only male or female flowers. Others have both male and female flowers. Palms are **pollinated** in many different ways.

Unlike the roots of trees, palm roots do not get thicker as they grow. Often, you can find a cone of roots at the base of a palm tree.

All of a palm's leaves grow at the top. Only a set number of leaves can grow on a palm. A new leaf does not begin to grow until an existing one dies.

In some palms, wind carries the **pollen**.
Bees, flies, beetles, and even bats pollinate other palms.
Palm **fruits** are usually berries with one **seed** or a fleshy fruit with one pit, or stone, inside. A coconut is an example of a fleshy palm fruit.

All-purpose plant

For hundreds of years, people living near palms have used them in many different ways. For example, palm trunks are used to construct buildings and furniture. Their leaves and husks are used to make ropes, mats, and thatched roofs. Parts of their fruits are used to make charcoal, cups, and bottles. Other fruits, such as dates, hearts of palm, and coconuts, are eaten as food. Their oils and juices are used in cooking. Palms are also used for decoration, especially in resorts along beaches.

The palm oil dilemma

Oil palms are one of many very useful palms. The fruit of these trees produces oil, which is used in a huge range of food in the developed world. However, there is a problem. In countries such as Indonesia and Sumatra, huge areas of rain forests—full of a wide variety of **species** of both plant and animal life—are being destroyed to make way for oil palm plantations. These **monocultures** are then at risk of disease, while rain forest plants are threatened with **extinction**.

Grasses, Sedges, and Their Relatives

Grasses, sedges, cattails, and other similar plants are also **monocots**. They all tend to have long, flat leaves and tall stems. These plants make small flowers without **nectar**. Their flowers are **pollinated** by wind.

Grasses

You are probably more familiar with grasses than you think. You see grasses growing on lawns and in parks. But did you know that you eat grass **fruits** every day? Rice, wheat, barley, rye, oats, and corn all come from grass plants. Cereal plants like these are the most important source of food in the world. About half of the energy that people get from food comes from grass plants.

Grasses spread easily and are hard to get rid of. Grasses can grow in areas too dry for trees and form grasslands, such as a prairie. Grasses can also **reproduce** through underground stems, called **rhizomes**. If the top of a grass plant is cut off by a lawn mower or by a grazing animal, it does not die. The part of the grass plant that grows is very low on the plant and is not disturbed by cutting the tips off.

Wheat flowers do not have petals or **sepals**. The grain is ground into flour, which is then used to make bread.

Sedges

Most sedges grow in wet places, such as on the shores of ponds and lakes and in marshes and swamps. Some sedges have stems and leaves that are hard to tear. They are used around the world to weave mats, baskets, and even to make sandals. Ancient Egyptians, Greeks, and Romans used a sedge plant, called papyrus, to make writing paper and books.

Sedges are the main plants in many wetlands around the world. Their fruits and other plant parts provide food for wetland animals. Their stems and leaves provide homes and hiding places for these animals.

Cattails

You have probably seen cattails growing beside a pond. Cattails have tall stems and long, flat leaves. Their leaves can be weaved into mats, baskets, and the seats of chairs. Cattail flowers have no petals at all. The brown part of a cattail contains the female flowers. The thinner, yellow part contains the male flowers. Wind or water carries cattail **seeds** to new places. All parts of cattails can be eaten. The yellow **pollen** of cattails can be added to cookie dough or pancake batter to make them taste better. Cattail stems can be used in salads. Their young green flower spikes can be cooked and eaten just like corn on the cob.

Worst weed in the world

Because sedges, such as this flea sedge, are good at growing in new places and can quickly spread out, they are common weeds. For example, purple nut sedge grows among crops in warm areas of the world. It is sometimes called the worst weed in the world because of all the damage it can cause.

You can tell sedges from grasses by cutting the stem across. When cut, a sedge stem end looks like a solid triangle. Grass stems usually look like hollow circles when cut in half.

Bromeliads, pineapples, bananas, ginger, and prayer plants are another group of **monocots**. Most bromeliads have short stems and pointed leaves with spines along the edges. The leaves overlap like the petals on a rose. Almost all bromeliads are native to North and South America and the West Indies.

Air plants

About half of all bromeliads are **epiphytes**, or air plants. Epiphytes are plants whose roots grow on other plants or in the air. They commonly grow in humid **climates**. Epiphytes are not **parasites**. They collect water from the plants they grow on in cuplike tanks formed by their leaves. The largest tank bromeliads hold as much as 20 liters (5 gallons) of water.

Bromeliads—mostly epiphytic American plants
- Often have flowers at the end of a long spike
- Leaves along spike are also brightly colored

The parts of a bromeliad

The roots of bromeliads that grow on rocks or on other plants hold the plant in place. These roots usually do not take in water or **nutrients** for the plant. Some bromeliads have no roots at all. The leaves of most epiphytic bromeliads do the job that roots normally do. They can take in water and nutrients. Bromeliads are **pollinated** mostly by hummingbirds. These birds are attracted to the flowers' **nectar**.

Bananas

Banana plants look like small trees, but they are not real trees. The part that looks like a trunk is made thick by layers of many large leaves. A large spike with many yellow flowers grows at the top of the plant and bends down toward the ground. One spike of flowers can grow into a bunch of 50–150 bananas. Each banana plant can produce only one bunch of bananas. Once a banana plant grows a bunch of bananas, the plant is usually cut down.

Bananas are one of the most important food crops in the world. Bananas are usually grown in warm areas, such as in Central and South America, and then shipped to markets in North America and around the world. Bananas are picked while they are still green so that they will become ripe after they arrive at the grocery store.

This frog has found a home in a water tank bromeliad.

Lilies, Orchids, and Their Relatives

Lilies, orchids, and their relatives form the largest group of **monocots**. Many of these plants have large, brightly colored flowers and sweet-smelling **nectar**. The flowers usually do not have green **sepals** under the flower petals. Instead, the sepals may resemble the petals. Animals usually **pollinate** these flowers. Leaves of these plants are long and thin and have parallel **veins**.

Members of this group include many familiar garden plants, such as irises, gladiolus, crocuses, narcissus, amaryllis, tulips, aloe plants, lilies, and orchids. Onion, garlic, leeks, shallots, and asparagus are plants in this group that are commonly eaten. Vanilla and saffron spices also come from plants in this group.

Underground parts

The underground parts of these plants mainly store food and water. **Rhizomes** and **corms** are underground stems. New plants can grow from these structures. For example, irises grow from rhizomes. Crocuses and gladiolus grow from corms.

This narcissus bulb is sprouting. The round part of the bulb at the bottom is made up of leaves that store food for the plant. The stems coming out of the top are the new growth.

Bulbs are round, underground buds surrounded by leaves. Onions are a good example of a bulb. The outside part of an onion is thin like paper. This papery covering protects the leaves inside. A bulb's leaves contain food that allows a plant to wait to grow until water is available. For example, during winter or when there is little rain, a bulb can feed itself until water becomes available.

Pollinators

Animals—mostly bees and other insects—commonly pollinate the flowers of orchids, lilies, and their relatives. Bees are attracted to the bright colors and sweet smells of the flowers. Some flowers even have nectar guides, which are special markings on flowers that direct bees to the **pollen** inside the flower. Birds sometimes pollinate a few plants in this group that have a distinctive flower pattern and color.

Orchids

The best place to find an orchid growing naturally is in a cloud forest. Cloud forests are wet and misty most of the time. This is the perfect climate for orchids, especially those growing on other plants. Orchid **epiphytes** take in water from the air.

This orchid looks similar to a female wasp. Male wasps pollinate the flowers when trying to mate with them.

The number of different types of living **organisms** in the world is often called the **biodiversity**. Sadly, all over the world, **species** of living organisms are becoming **extinct**. This means that these organisms no longer exist on Earth. There are many different reasons for this. Extinction has always happened— some species die out and other species **evolve**. But today people are changing the world in ways that affect all other species.

People are destroying the places where flowering plants live. We are cutting down rain forests and polluting air and water. Our use of fossil fuels, such as oil and gas, is causing global warming. Global warming is a rise in Earth's average temperature and a change in weather patterns. When the temperature and the weather change, it can have a serious effect on flowering plants.

Flowering plants have been on Earth a long time and are very important for people. We use them for food, for textiles (cotton and hemp), for construction (wood), for fuel (wood, biodiesel, ethanol from maize), and as medicines.

The demand of countries like ours for cheap food is driving the extinction of many flowering plants.

But the destruction of habitat by human activities is putting the survival of many species at risk. For example, rain forests are a treasure house of species. The warm, wet conditions mean many plants grow there that cannot survive anywhere else in the world. Many of these plants have not yet been identified—and some of them may well be very useful to humans. Unfortunately, rain forest is being destroyed at the rate of a small country every day, mainly for new farmland to grow crops, such as oil palms, or to feed cattle to provide cheap beef for burgers. Many flowering plants will become extinct before they have even been identified.

Seed banks—an investment for the future

Species of plants are becoming extinct all over the world due to changing environments and human activities. Seeds are a perfect way of preserving these threatened plants. They are small, and because plants make huge numbers of them, collecting seeds does not damage the natural populations. Once seeds have been dried and stored at low temperatures, they should survive for 200 years. Seed banks are being set up around the world with the aim of preserving as many species of flowering plants as possible. When the environment is less changeable once again, plants that have become extinct can be reintroduced into the wild.

What can be done?

To help prevent flowering plants from becoming extinct, people need to look after Earth better. If global warming can be stopped, many species will be saved. It is important to protect the places where flowering plants grow—which is almost everywhere. Biodiversity is important—we need as many species of plants as possible for the future.

Glossary

adaptation special feature that helps a plant survive in its habitat

ancestor plant relative that lived long ago

angiosperm flowering plant

bacteria single-celled organism that does not have a nucleus

biodiversity different types of organisms around the world

bulb underground resting form of a plant, which consists of a short stem with one or more buds surrounded by thick leaves

cell smallest unit of life

class level of classification that contains similar orders

classify group organisms into categories based on their similar characteristics

climate weather conditions that are usual for a certain area

complete flower flower that has sepals, petals, stamens, and pistils

corm short, swollen underground plant stem

cotyledon seed leaves a plant grows when it is still an embryo inside the seed

cultivated not wild or natural

deciduous loses leaves each year

dicot plant with two seed leaves

digest to break down food so it can be absorbed

digestive system group of organs that break down food so it can be used by the body

division level of classification that contains similar classes

embryo structure formed when an egg and a sperm join together

epiphyte any plant that grows on another plant or an object above ground and has no roots in soil

evolve change over time

extinct no longer on Earth

family level of classification that contains similar genera

fertilizing adding material to the soil to make it better able to produce

fossil remains of an ancient living organism found in rocks

fruit enlarged female reproductive part of a flowering plant. It contains and protects the seeds of flowering plants.

fungi any of a large group of plantlike organisms that must live on other plants or animals or decaying material

gene structure by which all living things pass on characteristics to the next generation

genetic to do with the makeup of an organism

genus (plural is **genera**) level of classification that contains similar species

gymnosperm earliest seed plants

habitat place where an organism lives

host plant on which a parasite lives and feeds from

imperfect flower flower that has only female or male reproductive parts

incomplete flower missing either sepals, petals, stamens, or pistils

kingdom level of classification that contains similar phyla or divisions

mineral solid substance formed in the earth by nature

monocot plant with one seed leaf

monoculture when one single crop is grown on the same land

nectar sweet liquid produced by some flowers

nitrogen colorless, odorless gaseous chemical element that makes up 78 percent of the atmosphere and forms a part of all living tissue

nutrient chemical that helps plants grow and carry out life processes

order level of classification that contains similar families

organism living thing

parasite living thing that lives and feeds on or inside another living thing

perfect flower flower that has both male and female reproductive parts

photosynthesis process by which plants use carbon dioxide in the air and energy from sunlight to make food in the form of sugars

phylum (plural is **phyla**) level of classification that contains similar classes

pistil female reproductive part of a flower

pollen dustlike particles that contain sperm

pollination transfer of pollen from male to female flower parts

predator animal that hunts and eats other animals

prey animal that is hunted and eaten by other animals

reproduce produce another living thing of the same kind

rhizome underground stem that looks like a root and holds the plant in the soil

seed structure that contains an undeveloped plant and stored food that the plant needs to grow

sepal part of a flower that surrounds and protects the flower before it blooms

species level of classification that contains similar organisms

stamen male reproductive part of a flower

tuber short, fleshy underground stem

vein bundle of tubes in a leaf that transports water and nutrients

whorl sepals, petals, stamens, and/or pistils

Find Out More

Burnie, David. *Plant* (e.guides). New York: DK Children, 2006.

Burnie, David. *The Concise Nature Encyclopedia*. Boston, Mass.: Kingfisher, 2006.

Hunter, Rebecca. *The Facts About Flowering Plants*. Danbury, Conn.: Franklin Watts, 2007.

Index